Jada and Grandpa Talk Coconuts

Layout and Design by DaSum Company LLC

Copyright © 2017 by Fay Taylor

Taylor Productions

ISBN-13 - 978-0-9800468-2-3
ISBN-10 - 09800468-2-3

Credits

Cover by Debbie Tosun Kilday.

Editing by Roberta Buland and Vangella 'Vjange Hazle' Buchanan.

Picture of coconut tree on the cover by Alvajoy Cain.

Some pictures taken by Alvajoy Cain, Monique Taylor, Fay Taylor, Kay Taylor–Brooks, Rudolph Brooks, Shirley Fagon, Geraldine Sayers Lindo, Sean Taylor.

Final book layout, Dan Uitti.

Note from the author

The uses of the coconut are endless. Different countries have their own inventions for each part of the coconut. Some of the information mentioned in this book is from Jamaica and is based on the experience and memory of the author who grew up in the Caribbean island.

Photo 1. Jada and Grandpa

Grandpa Taylor received a gift from Uncle Tony. The gift was coconuts he brought from Florida. Uncle Tony knew Grandpa Taylor loved coconuts. The coconuts' colors were green and gold, and were picked from the coconut tree, which is also called the coconut palm. Jada was filled with curiosity as she watched Grandpa Taylor, whom she called Papa, chop the coconuts with a large knife he called a machete. She questioned him about them. He told her everything he knew about the coconut.

He explained that it was a hard-shelled fruit with many different parts and many uses.

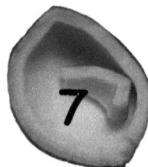

Photo 2. The coconut tree or coconut palm—showing Tall and Short.

"There are two types of coconut trees; most are very tall, and some are short," Papa explained to Jada. "The short ones are called Dwarf Coconut trees. These trees grow in Africa, also in tropical countries such as India, Mexico, the Philippines, and islands like Barbados and Jamaica in the Caribbean where Grandma and I were born. Two tropical places in the United States of America where they grow are Hawaii and Florida."

Papa said that there are also two stages for the coconuts: the young one and the mature one.

Photo 3. Young and mature coconuts

Photo 4. Dry coconut

"The coconut changes color according to its stages. In its young stage, the color is green; as it matures, the color turns gold. Then, when it gets dry, it turns brown."

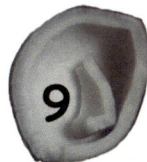

9

Photo 5. Cut Jelly, round coconut and husk

The first coconut that Papa showed Jada was the young coconut, which is called Jelly Coconut because the meat inside is soft like jelly. He cut the top off with his machete and poured the water from it into a glass then told her to taste it.

Photo 6. Coconut water

"Papa," Jada asked, "how did the water get inside of the coconut?"

"Coconuts have water inside; but no one knows how the coconut water gets inside while they are growing on the trees. You can also drink the coconut water straight from the coconut but it is easier to pour it into a container or drink it with a straw," he answered.

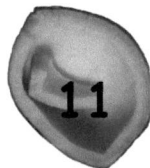

11

Photo 7. Aunt Kay

Aunt Kay enjoying the jelly meat with a spoon cut from the outer shell of the coconut.

He told her of some of the benefits of the coconut water:

Coconut water is fat free and has less sugar than some juices and sodas. It is good for you, especially in the summertime because it will quench your thirst.

Papa said that the drier coconuts, which are the more mature ones, have the sweeter water. Therefore, the water in the jelly coconuts is not as sweet as the water in the mature ones.

He wanted her to taste the jelly inside of the coconut. To get to the soft meat, he first chopped the coconut open using a sharp machete, and then he scraped the jelly out with a spoon for her to taste it. "When someone buys a jelly coconut, the men who cut it open usually make a spoon by cutting a piece from the outer shell to eat the jelly meat," he explained.

Jada's Aunt Kay loves the jelly meat and the coconut water so whenever she travels to tropical places she always buys a jelly coconut.

Photo 8. Eden

Photo 9. Split coconut

While on vacation with her parents, Jada's cousin Eden taste coconut water for the first time.

Papa then showed Jada the mature coconut. It has two hard shells, the outer shell and the inner shell. This outer shell is called the husk. The inner shell is brown and houses the white, hard meat inside.

The soft jelly meat becomes hard when the coconut is mature. This meat is grated and squeezed with water to extract the milk.

Photo 10. Grating or shredding the coconut

When Grandma Taylor was a young girl in Jamaica, she grated the coconut on a metal grater by hand. Now, there are machines such as blenders that will grate or shred it much faster. The grated part is called the coconut trash and the liquid from it is called coconut milk. It looks like cow's milk but does not taste that way. The grated coconut, before removing the milk, can be used for baking and making snacks called Grater Cake. After the milk is squeezed out, the coconut trash can be used for feeding chickens.

15

The coconut meat, when cut into small pieces, makes snacks called Cut Cakes or Coconut Drops. Adding sugar to the cut pieces and boiling it makes the Cut Cakes or Drops. They are called Drops because they are spooned and dropped onto a surface until they cool and harden and are ready to eat. The Grater Cake is made from the coconut trash, mixed with sugar, and boiled. This is also then dropped onto a surface until cooled for a sweet, delicious treat. The coconut meat can also be eaten as it is removed from the shell.

Photo 11. Picture of grater cake

Photo 12. Coconut Cut Cake or Drops

Coconut milk is not the same as the coconut water. While the coconut water is the clear liquid you see when the coconut is first cut open, the milk comes from grating the coconut, pouring water on the trash, and squeezing it through a strainer.

Photo 13. Coconut trash and strainer

Photo 14. Coconut milk

The milk is used to make oil by boiling the milk for a long time until it changes to oil. The oil floats on top of a creamy like substance called Custard. Freshly made oil is liquid but solidifies when it is cold. The oil is used for cooking or baking and the custard can be eaten as is. It can also be used to make a dish called Run-dung. Add fish, mainly mackerel, with seasonings such as onions and peppers into the custard to cook. It is delicious as a snack or a meal.

Photo 15. Liquid Coconut Oil

Photo 16. Solid Coconut Oil.

Using coconut oil has many natural benefits. You can use it as lip balm to protect your lips from dryness, as massage oil to soothe sore muscles, and as hair conditioner that leaves your hair healthy. Coconut milk is also used for cooking tasty dishes such as rice and peas and stewed peas. Grandma Taylor makes the best rice and peas; anyone who ever tasted it, loves it.

Photo 17. Grandma Taylor's Rice and Peas

As Papa removed the husk to get to the inner part, he explained to her that every part of the coconut is useful and is used to provide food, drink, shelter and animal feed. Jada was even more curious about this unusual fruit; the more

Papa explained the more she wanted to know. She was amazed when he removed the inner coconut that she was not aware of. It was round as a ball with three eyes that gave it the resemblance of a monkey's face. It had water inside like the jelly coconut had.

Papa pierced one of the eyes and water came squirting out. Jada jumped back.

"This is also where the new coconut plant begins," Papa explained.

Papa had to use his hammer to break this inner coconut shell because it was very hard.

Photo 18. Inner coconut with shell

After the meat is removed from the inner shell, the shell is transformed into different products such as utensils, cups, dolls, musical instruments and jewelry.

Photo 19. Some products made from coconut

Some cultures use the dry husk, which is brown color to make brushes for cleaning floors; it gives the floor a beautiful shine. Fiber from the husk is made into stuffing for the mattresses.

Photo 17. Coconut Husk

Photo 20. Coconut Brush

Grandpa Taylor told Jada how he would climb the tall coconut trees to pick the coconuts when he lived in Jamaica. This led him to inform her about uses of the tree.

Photo 21. Climbing a coconut tree

"From the trunk of the tree they make wood, which is then made into floorboards and furniture. The leaves are used to make fans, mats, hats, brooms and roof for huts. The vane in the middle of the leaf is used to make kites. As a boy, I flew many a kite with long tails whistling in the wind."

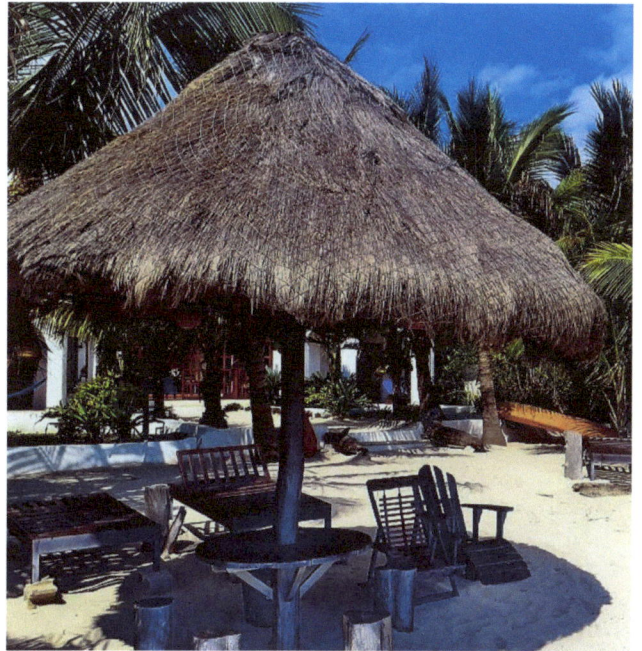

Photo 22. Outdoor Umbrella manufactured from the leaves

Coconut trees also bloom flowers. The insects and the wind carry pollen from the male flower to the female flower.

Even the roots are used to make dye, toothbrush, mouthwash and some medicine.

These are some of the reasons the coconut is called *The Tree of Life*.

"Wow!" Jada exclaimed. "This is awesome, Papa."

Papa smiled, his mind on the memories of boyhood days on a tropical island eating the fruit of the coconut tree and drinking the water from the coconut.

Review Questions

1. Have you ever seen a real coconut?

2. Describe it.

3. Based on the pictures in the book are you able to recognize a coconut?

4. Have you ever tasted a coconut?

5. Have you ever tasted coconut water or coconut milk?

6. If so, describe the taste.

7. Name one place where coconut trees are grown.

8. Name some things that are made from the coconut and the coconut tree.

9. How is coconut oil made?

10. How is coconut milk made?

11. What are the colors of the coconuts?

Photo 23. Jada with her Grandpa

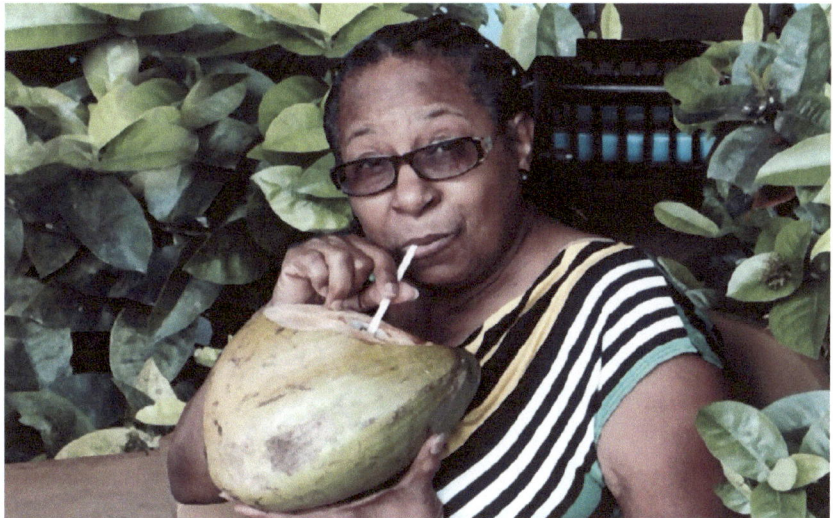

Photo 24. Author Grandma Fay drinking from the coconut

www.ingramcontent.com/pod-product-compliance
Lightning Source LLC
Chambersburg PA
CBHW042118040426
42449CB00002B/94